The Ayurvedic Cookbook

The Ayurvedic Cookbook

Get Fit in Just Two Weeks

Gita Ramesh

Photographs by
Sanjay Ramachandran

Lustre Press
Roli Books

Contents

Introduction

Having authored the book on "Ayurvedic Herbal Massage" which was at a time when neither people were aware of what Ayurveda was nor were there many books available in English on the subject. I saw a need to write a more simplified version of what Ayurveda is. The final product, a pictorial book, was well accepted and received a lot of acclaim.

Thereafter, my husband and I wanted to set up a place where one could avail such treatments in a serene, calm and effective environment. This was when a lifestyle management centre called Kairali – The Ayurvedic Healing Village – came about. Here, food was an integral part of the Ayurvedic treatments offered. Our guests came from far and wide like Japan, United States, Germany, France, Russia, Australia, Middle East and, of course, people from all across India. It was a pleasure to see so many people across so many different nationalities coming to experience the wonders of our Indian science "Ayurveda".

Developing dishes according to taste and likings of different cultures was a very important and a challenging task. Keeping in mind that the dishes selected were what people knew and loved. Changing them to a more suitable and healthier version with local ingredients proved an uphill task. Most of us know the nutritional values and health aspects of different foods. This knowledge and wisdom is always passed from mother to child, advising which food should be eaten and which to be avoided. An Indian kitchen acts as a medicine cabinet, with many homemade remedies. I would like to impart all this knowledge, which I acquired over the years, through this book.

In Ayurveda, every human being is a unique combination of five elements provided to us by Mother Nature: Water, Earth, Fire, Air and Ether. In Ayurveda, there are three primary life forces in the body or three biological humors. These are called *Vata*, *Pitta* and *Kapha*. *Vata* denotes Ether and Air, *Pitta* stands for Fire and *Kapha* is Water and Earth.

Keeping all this in mind, I worked on our recipes to suit all body types whether it was *Vata*, *Pitta* or *Kapha*. The aim was to offer our guests a balanced diet, maintain their health and to satisfy their needs, especially for guests that stayed with us for over two or three weeks! We had one rule – food was not

Divine Destination where nature nurtures your well being.

to be repeated. Hence, adding variety was essential, keeping in mind both the nutritional and medicinal value, as well as retaining its flavour and looking into availability of seasonal vegetables and fruits. This resulted in creating a healthy and interesting menu for the Resort.

Ayurveda suggests/states that while undergoing treatments one should be vegetarian and the food should be healthy, freshly cooked and easily digestible. Fresh organic food contains the maximum natural vitamins. No preserved food or artificial colouring is used in any of our dishes. Absolutely no cream or nut paste is used, and just the right amount of oil is added in all our recipes, only what is essential for the body and mind.

After the overwhelming response from our guests, and encouragement from my family and relatives, I decided to take time out and write this book. It is heartfelt and touching when you hear people say that I was responsible for the betterment or positive change in their lives. Some even converted into being pure vegetarians after staying with us. The knowledge that vegetarian food can be good and there is variety in it was completely lacking which had to be changed. People did not know that they could have three proper square meals that were vegetarian and still be able to live healthy and lose weight – no dieting required. Their skin could look fabulous, well toned and nourished just with a few minor adjustments in their daily diet.

"The Ayurvedic Cookbook", I think, is not only for my guests visiting our Resort, but for anyone who wants to live healthy and eat healthy.
Anybody with absolutely no cooking skills can follow these simple and quick recipes and eat fresh and hot food.

Traditional Ayurvedic therapy rooms to revitalize the mind, body and soul.

Ash gourd (white pumpkin): This vegetable contains plenty of water wih zero fat content. It has enormous medicinal properties and is used in Ayurvedic therapies. Being low in calories, it is an ideal vegetable for diabetic patients and is good for weight control. In Ayurveda, the juice of ash gourd is used effectively in mercury poisoning and snakebites.

Aubergine, Eggplant (brinjal): It contains some essential nutrients that are highly beneficial for the human body. It is light in digestion, acts as a purgative and helps in obesity. The fruit is rich in dietary fibre, vitamins and minerals. The vitamins it contains are several like vitamin C, thiamine, riboflavin, niacin, etc.

Baby corn: Low in fat, baby corn is a good source of potassium, vitamin C and fibre. Being high in fibre, it prevents constipation and colon cancer. It holds a great degree of nutritional value and has numerous health benefits. Baby corn contains some carotenoids which help in the promotion of eye-health.

Baby onion: This vegetable is best for diseases like cold, asthma and respiratory problems. The onion is known for its curative value from ancient times. Consuming onion juice mixed with honey can relive sore throat and cough symptoms. The juice can also be used for earaches.

Banana: Good for people who are anemic, banana contains high levels of iron and can stimulate the production of haemoglobin in the blood. It is extremely high in potassium yet low in salt hence, very good for blood pressure. It helps to overcome constipation.

Banana stem: This is supposed to be the waste of the plant yet it is very good for health. It has very high nutritive value. It adds bulk to the food and is very useful for those wanting to reduce weight. The fibre in it helps to overcome constipation and it also helps to detoxify the body.

Beetroot: High in nutrients like vitamin C and iron, beetroot helps in absorbing iron from the body. It is best eaten raw as vitamin C is water soluble hence, if you cook the beetroot, it loses its vitamin content.

Bitter gourd: This is one vegetable that can help your body be disease free, due to its disease preventing and health promoting phyto chemical compound. As its name suggests, it is one of the most bitter of all culinary vegetables. It is very low in calories, but rich in dietary fibre, minerals, vitamins and antioxidants.

Black currant: This fruit has a lot of therapeutic value and contains complex vitamins like vitamin C, potassium salts and essential oils. This fruit is also considered to be an elixir of youth. It is a good diuretic and has anti-rheumatic effects and helps in the elimination of uric acid.

Bottle gourd: One of the most common vegetables in India, bottle gourd has a lot of health benefits. It is very good for high blood pressure and heart diseases. It is considered to be good for weight reduction as it contains 90% water and is very low in calories.

Broccoli: It belongs to the same family as cauliflower and like cauliflower it is low in fat and can fight against cancer. Broccoli contains vitamin C and K. It also provides fibre, folate, manganese and beta–carotene. This vegetable helps protect from prostate cancer, stroke risks and eye diseases.

Cabbage: It is an excellent source of vitamin C, which is one of the best antioxidants and helps in reducing the aging process. It is also good for constipation. It helps in stomach ulcers, excess weight, skin disorders, eczema, rheumatism, arthritis, gout and eye disorders and in proper functioning of the nervous system.

Capsicum: It holds a great degree of nutritional value and has numerous health benefits. Capsicum is a very good source of vitamins A, B and C and minerals like calcium and potassium. It is also good for weight reduction.

Carrot: A good source of fibre, carrot is an amazing vegetable and easy to add to your diet. It slows down the ageing of cells, is excellent for the eyes and contains a large quantity of vitamin A in the form of beta-carotene. It also has cancer-curing properties.

Cauliflower: It is low in fat and carbohydrates but high in dietary fibre, folate and vitamin C. Possessing high nutritional value, cauliflower is beneficial to human health. It is very helpful to those suffering from prostate, breast, cervical, colon and ovarian cancer as it contains several anti-cancer phyto-chemicals.

Celery: It is an important medicinal plant, which helps in curing various health disorders. It helps in arthritis, rheumatism, liver disorders, etc. Celery contains minerals, vitamins and its oil has specific effect on the regulation of nervous system with great calming influences. It also helps to reduce high blood pressure.

Coconut: This fruit has many health benefits with amazing medicinal properties. The water is a natural drink for hydration and is high in energy. Its edible flesh is part of the daily diet of people in Kerala and is used in most of their dishes. It is rich in fibre, minerals and vitamins and has more than 90% saturated fats.

Coriander leaves: These leaves when digested turns sweet and alleviates irritation in the intestine. They have magnesium, potassium and fibre in plenty. Regular consumption boosts immunity and purifies blood. This is one herb that is widely cultivated in India. It is also a great herb for skin, to treat pimples and blackheads.

Cucumber: It has many health benefits that is why it is one of the most important part of the food diet as well as the skin diet. It is soothing and softening for the skin and very cooling for the eyes. (Regular intake of cucumber juice is very beneficial both internally and externally.) It contains almost 90% water hence, the juice is good for weight reduction.

Curry leaves: An aromatic herb, curry leaves are a unique flavouring agent. The leaves' benefits are not just for its taste, but it is also used as a natural remedy for many health conditions and disorders. It is believed that eating few fresh curry leaves daily manages diabetes, reduces cholesterol, aids in weight loss and prevents early development of cataract.

Drumstick: Many of the medicinal and nutritional properties of drumstick have long been known in India. Due to its high iron content, it is very beneficial for many ailments. It contains digestible protein, calcium, iron, vitamin C and carotenoids. Almost all parts of the drumstick tree has medicinal value.

Drumstick Leaves: The drumstick leaves are not only relished as a vegetable, but are used in treatments too for its medicinal value. They are used in treatment of rheumatism, and are a good circulatory stimulant. The leaves are used in the poultice for reducing glandular swelling.

French beans: Fresh French beans are very low in fat and a good source of vitamins and minerals. They act as a laxative and help in good digestion. These beans are very good antioxidants and contain excellent levels of vitamins A and C which help the body to develop resistance against infection.

Gherkin: It is rich in fibre and has a high percentage of water. The fibre helps in cleaning the digestive track and in the smooth functioning of the digestive system. It is rich in vitamin C and helps in various skin disorders. Gherkin helps in reducing blood pressure due to its content of potassium and magnesium.

Goosberry: This fruit is an indispensable part of the Ayurvedic medicine. Gooseberry has amazing remedial qualities and is basically sour. It is rich in vitamin C and helps in lowering the blood pressure. It has anti-diabetic quality. It also helps in promoting hair growth and is one of the best antioxidant fruits.

Grapes: This fruit has many medicinal values and is rich in nutrients. It helps to prevent blood clots and the antioxidants in the grapes help to stop the oxidation of the bad cholesterol. Grapes contain flavonoids which help to reduce the effects of aging. Grapes are sweet and slightly sour making them a useful liver tonic.

Green peas: They are one of the most nutritious, leguminous vegetables, rich in minerals, vitamins and antioxidants. Green peas are relatively low in calories and have no cholesterol. They are a good source of protein and contain soluble as well as insoluble fibre. Green peas are an excellent source of folic acid, vitamins C, K and A.

Guava: It is one of the richest source of dietary fibre. Guava seeds serve as an excellent laxative. It has a rich source of iron which is proven to be preventive against cold and viral infections. It is very rich in vitamins, keeps the skin glowing and prevents aging.

Lime: This fruit is not only used for culinary purpose but also for cosmetic and medicinal purposes. It contains water soluble vitamin C which is very good for the blood vessels, muscles and cartilage. It also has anti-cancer properties and is a natural cure for diseases like scurvy.

Long beans: This is one vegetable that is available throughout the year. They are low in calories and hence can be consumed by those on a diet. It is considered to be an energy food. Being green in colour it is rich in phyto chemicals and antioxidants and can fight cancer and delay aging.

Mint: This is a herb with remarkable medicinal properties. It is used in various products from toothpaste to candies and also in our daily food. It promotes digestion and is a good appetizer. The strong and refreshing aroma of mint is an excellent quick remedy for nausea, respiratory disorders and cold and cough. It is an excellent skin cleanser.

Okra: This is a very low-calorie vegetable containing no saturated fats or cholesterol. It is rich in dietary fibre, minerals and vitamins, and is highly recommended for weight reduction and cholesterol control programs. A good source of calcium and potassium, okra helps to stabilize the blood sugar.

Onion: Its nutritional value has been evident for many generations and is being used for thousands of years. It is used as a diuretic, for digestion, for the heart, eyes and joints. It is low in fat, calories and is cholesterol free. Onion extract is very good for prevention of arthritis, cough and cold, asthma and bronchitis.

Papaya: It is a rich and powerful source of antioxidant and contains carotenes, vitamins C, B and E and minerals like potassium and magnesium. It helps prevent cancer and is very good for digestive disorders. It is believed to be one of the best for premature aging.

Pomegranate: This fruit has been widely used in Ayurveda for various remedies down the ages. It is very effective in reducing heart diseases, in lowering blood pressure and has antioxidant properties. It also lowers the risk of cancer and controls weight. Pomegranate is a good blood thinner.

Potato: Rich in several micro-nutrients especially vitamin C, potato has a moderate source of iron. The vitamin C content promotes iron absorption. It is a good source of vitamin B1, B3 and B6 and minerals such as potassium, phosphorus, etc. Potato also contains dietary antioxidants which may play a part in preventing diseases related to aging.

Raw banana: Like potato, raw banana is used in main course for its source of carbohydrates. The dietary fibre helps in normal bowel movements and in reducing constipation. The potassium in it helps to control heart rate and blood pressure, countering negative effects of sodium. It is also beneficial for our brains and kidneys.

Red amaranth: This vegetable is recommended for people who have low red blood cell count. It also prevents and treats hypertension and cardiovascular disease. Regular consumption can reduce cholesterol levels and lower blood pressure. These leaves are a good home remedy for hair loss and premature greying.

Red cabbage: Like the green cabbage, it has similar properties. It is both fat free and cholesterol free. Rich in vitamin C, red cabbage has shown to have disease preventive properties. The red colour is due to certain flavonoids which act as anti-inflammatory.

Red long beans: This beans is a perfect food for reducing weight. It is low in fat content and is a rich source of protein and fibre which helps to lower the higher cholesterol level in the blood system. It is also rich in vitamins A, B, C and E and are an excellent source of calcium, iron and potassium.

Red radish: Like the white radish, red radish too has very high nutritional value. It is rich in ascorbic acid, folic acid and potassium. A good source of vitamin B6, riboflavin, magnesium, copper and calcium, red radish regularizes the metabolism of the body.

Spinach: Highly nutritious, the calcium content in spinach helps to strengthen the bones. The vitamins, fibre content, folic acids and minerals in them helps control cancer. The folate in it helps in protection against heart diseases. It is also good in preventing memory loss.

Star fruit: Rich in vitamins A and C as well as potassium, phosphorous, iron and calcium, star fruit is a good source of fibre, amino acids and antioxidants. The skin of the fruit is rich in tannin which regulates the intestine. It is also known to be effective in hormone regulation. Star fruit is a popular remedy for curing hangovers.

Tomato: This is one vegetable that is routinely used in the Indian kitchen. It not only has nutrients like calcium and sulphur with medicinal values but it is full of micro-nutrients and minerals that are essential for maintenance of body and its growth. It is very low in any fat contents and has zero cholesterol levels.

Watermelon: It is an excellent source for vitamins A and C. Vitamin A is important for healthy eyes. The vitamin B6 found in watermelon helps the immune system produce antibodies which are needed to fight diseases. It is an important fruit to be added to the weight reduction diet.

White radish: It contains a lot of juice and is both sweet and pungent in taste. It has very rich roughage and hence, facilitates digestion and cures constipation. It is very good for those suffering from piles. It also helps in urinary disorders. This vegetable is good for weight reduction.

Yam: A good source of energy, yam contains complex carbohydrates and soluble dietary fibre. This vegetable has been used in traditional medicine for a very long time. It reduces water retention and helps in heart conditions. It also aids digestion and stimulates bile flow.

Yellow pumpkin: A wild growing vegetable, yellow pumpkin is incredibly rich in vital antioxidants and vitamins. This like the white pumpkin is a low-calorie vegetable, rich in dietary fibre and minerals. It is one of the best vegetables in controlling weight and cholesterol.

Asafoetida: It aids enormously in the digestion of a meal. It is a pungent, resinous gum used and held in great esteem amongst indigenous medicines from earliest times in India. It expels wind from the stomach and is a sedative. It is used as an antibiotic, by protecting one from diseases. It also treats bronchitis.

Barley: A healthier high-fibre, high protein whole grain, barley has numerous health benefits. It reduces the risk of heart diseases and lowers cholesterol. As barley is extremely low in calories, it acts as a wonderful diet supplement and helps to maintain a slim stature.

Black pepper: It is pungent and offers warmth to any curry. Black pepper is one of the oldest and most important of all spices. It is a stimulant, aromatic, digestive and a nervine tonic. It has a stimulating effect on the digestive organ and is a good home remedy for digestive disorders.

Chickpea: This is very high in protein and is a good source of zinc and folate. It is one of the key ingredients of a cuisine in India and a healthy addition to any diet. Chickpea is naturally low in fat, high in dietary fibre and rich in vitamins and minerals.

Cinnamon: One of the oldest spices, cinnamon is used in medicine and in cooking. It makes the food tastier with its extraordinary smell. It helps to lower cholesterol and can regulate the effect on blood sugar. It helps in arthritis pain as it is a high source of manganese, fibre, iron and calcium.

Clove: Used for centuries for its medicinal value and as a nutritional spice for food, clove is high in many minerals. It is analgesic and has anti-inflammatory and anti-bacterial effects with a distinct aromatic smell. It is very good for toothaches. Its antiseptic properties help to reduce infections.

Coriander seeds: They possess ample nutritional as well as medicinal properties, and are one of the most commonly used seeds. They are used for many medicinal purposes. The seeds can be soaked in water, strained and then used for washing the eyes. It cools the eyes and removes fatigue.

Cumin seeds: Cumin has been in use since ancient times as a spice for their distinctive flavour and aroma. A very warm spice, cumin is slightly bitter in taste. It is very useful in digestive disorders. In Ayurveda, cumin seed water is given after intake of meals, which enhances digestion and is antiseptic.

Curd: It is sour in taste and is used to treat diarrhea and dysentery. It causes heaviness when used in excess and can lead to constipation. It accelerates digestion, acts as an appetizer and is a nutritious food option for all ages. Curd is rich in calcium, protein, riboflavin and vitamins.

Dry red chilli: It contains vitamin C and carotene in hugh amounts. It has many health benefits and is good for stimulating appetite and for boosting blood circulation. A small amount of red chilli is recommended in the diet to boost the immune system.

Fenugreek: A bitter, pungent, sweet and warming, fenugreek is a good rejuvenator and very good for diabetes too. The regular use of fenugreek helps to keep the body clean and healthy. It can lower cholesterol levels and improve digestion. It is very good for skin problems. It is packed with vitamins A, B, C and E. It also has anti-aging properties.

Garlic: This has been medicinally used for many years for various diseases and is one of the most valuable ingredients added in various dishes. It is very good for heart patients as it reduces the cholesterol level. It also reduces the risk of cancer and helps in weight loss. Two drops of garlic oil helps to cure earaches.

Ghee: This is clarified butter and is commonly used in Indian cooking. It is the main ingredient in some of the Ayurvedic medicines. It is also used for various treatments when combined with a variety of herbs especially in cases of ulcer and constipation.

Ginger: Hot and pungent, ginger is stimulating to both digestion and circulation. It is excellent for cold and cough. As the case with most spices, ginger also has aphrodisiac properties. It is widely used as a local medicine and is high in vitamin C.

Green chilli: It has disease preventing and health promoting properties. Green chilli is the staple food of Indian cuisine. Rich in vitamin C, vitamin A and flavonoids, green chilli also contains minerals like potassium, manganese, iron and magnesium.

Green gram, sprouted: Sprouted green gram is one of the most nutritious gram and promotes well being (its nutritional value increases when sprouted). Its soup speeds recovery from acute diseases. It acts as the best anti-bacterial soap. It removes the dirt from the skin without causing any irritation.

Fennel: It cools and sweetens the curry. Fennel is often used as a mouth freshener or as a digestive aid after meals. If used in excess it will dominate the curry. It is appetizing, stimulating, a good laxative and has aphrodisiac properties.

Jaggery: This is obtained from plant and does not involve any chemicals hence, all the natural mineral salts are retained in jaggery. It is known to have various medicinal properties and health benefits. It also treats problems such as dry cough, common cold and asthma. It is very rich in iron.

Mustard seeds: It is a warmth-giving herb with a pungent taste and is mildly diuretic. These seeds have not only been used as a spice but also in medicines since ancient times. The seeds are high in essential oil and in calories. The oil has traditionally been used to relieve muscle pain, rheumatic and arthritic pains.

Navara rice: This rice has antioxidant properties and is rich in minerals, iron and zinc. It rectifies the basic ills effecting the circulatory, respiratory and digestive systems. This rice can be consumed internally too and has been identified as a rice protein that is reportedly an anti-cancer agent, particularly effective against breast cancer.

Nutmeg: It is used as a preventive and healing medicine. Medically it has strong anti-bacterial properties. Nutmeg is effective in killing a number of cavity-causing bacteria in the mouth. It is used as a medicine to improve memory. It reduces flatulence, aids digestion and improves appetite.

Oats: High source of vitamins, oats has a good balance of essential fatty acids, which are lined with longevity and general good health. It also contains hundreds of phyto-chemicals which help to reduce the risk of cancer.

Peanut: This nut is enriched with noteworthy health benefiting nutrients. Rich in energy, peanut contains minerals, antioxidants and vitamins. This nut is an excellent source of vitamin E.

Prunus cerasoides (Himalayan wild cherries / *pathumukham*): It pacifies the burning sensation in the body and has many health benefits. It also has antioxidant properties.

Ragi: A wonder grain with numerous health benefits. It is rich in calcium, but higher in proteins and minerals. It is rich in fibre and, therefore, suitable for people trying to lose weight.

Rock salt: This salt has many benefits, besides being used in cooking it is used for its medicinal value as well as for beauty treatments. Regular use of this salt in cooking can control all health problems. It can also be used as a body scrub and a teeth whitener.

Sago: Sago is a common ingredient used in Indian recipes. It provides a lot of energy and is very low in calorie. It is a good substitute for rice, as a light meal portion, and good for weight reduction.

Tamarind: This is used in Ayurvedic medicines and as a mild laxative. As it is acidic it excites the bile and other juices in the body. It is also used as a blood purifier and is sweet and tangy in taste. Its pulp is made into a liquid and administered to alleviate alcoholic intoxication.

Tribulus Terrestis (land caltrops / *nerinjil*): This is one of the most common herb for healing used in Ayurveda. It can treat various urinary problems and urinary stone, eye problems, pre-menstrual syndrome and high blood pressure.

Tulsi: This herb has many remedies for a lot of common ailment. The leaves are a nerve tonic and also sharpens the memory. Tulsi is very good for cough and cold. Its juice mixed with honey helps to expel kidney stones. It relieves stress and increases immunity and has rejuvenating properties.

Turmeric: One of most fundamental spice that is often used in not only Ayurvedic cooking but practically in all Indian cooking. Turmeric is pungent, bitter and slightly astringent. It is an excellent blood purifier and anti-inflammatory. Its bright colour gives curries their characteristic hue. It is a very useful antiseptic which helps in the intestinal lining disorders.

White dal: This is known as *urad dal*, it is rich in vitamins, minerals and dietary fibre. It contains plenty of potassium and helps in reducing high blood pressure.

Salads

Salads, one of the most essential part of our diet, has plenty of health benefits. Eating salad every day is a healthy habit that one can adopt. It is also very easy to prepare. Eating fibre-rich salad makes one feel fuller. Thus one tends to eat less resulting in weight reduction.

The salad recipes mentioned here contain not only vegetables, but fruits as well.

Vegetables like carrot, beetroot, radish and fruits like pomegranate, papaya, watermelon and banana are all healthy and nutritious.

Seasonal Fruits organically grown in Kairali – The Ayurvedic Healing Village – to give the required nutrients to our system.

Carrot Black Currant Salad

Serves 2-3 Persons

Ingredients
½ cup / 100 gm black currants (*munakka*)
5-6 carrots (*gajar*), medium-sized
½ cup / 100 gm celery, chopped
½ tsp / 2½ ml honey
½ tsp / 2½ ml lime (*nimbu*) juice
a pinch salt

Method
Soak the black currants in boiling water for about 5-10 minutes; strain and keep aside.
Wash the carrots thoroughly and peel the outer layer. Now grate the carrots and put into a salad bowl along with celery, honey, lime juice and salt; toss well.
Now add the black currants and serve in a plate with a wedge of lime.

Beetroot and Gherkin Salad

Serves 2-3 Persons

Ingredients

1 beetroot (*chukandar*), large
4 gherkins
1 green chilli, small, finely chopped
½ tsp / 2½ ml lime (*nimbu*) juice
Salt to taste
some coriander (*dhaniya*) leaves, fresh, chopped

Method

Steam the beetroot and gherkins. Peel the beetroot and cut into thin strips. Put into a bowl.
Slice the steamed gherkins and add to the beetroot strips.
Add the green chilli, lime juice and salt; toss well.
Serve garnished with fresh coriander leaves.

Garden Fresh Salad

Serves 2-3 Persons

Ingredients

3 tomatoes, sliced
1 cucumber (*khira*), medium-sized, sliced
2 red radish (*lal mooli*), medium-sized, sliced with skin
1 stalk celery, shredded
½ tsp / 2½ ml lime (*nimbu*) juice
Salt to taste

Method

Lay the tomatoes on a plate topped with a layer of cucumber and then radish.
Decorate the salad with shredded celery.
Add lime juice and salt to taste; serve.

Sprouted Green Gram Salad

Serves 2-3 Persons

Ingredients
1 cup / 200 gm sprouted green gram (*moong*)
1 onion, chopped
1 tomato, chopped
1 green chilli, chopped
Salt to taste
¼ **tsp** cumin (*jeera*) seeds, roasted, powdered
½ tsp / 2½ ml lime (*nimbu*) juice
a few coriander (*dhaniya*) leaves, finely chopped

Method
Fresh sprouted green gram can be prepared at home. Take a handful of green gram, wash thoroughly and soak in a container till it absorbs a good quantity of water. Drain the water out and transfer the green gram into a sprouting container. Allow it to stand for about 3-4 days.

Now wash and drain the sprouts, steam for 5-7 minutes and put into a bowl.

Add the onion, tomato, green chilli and salt; mix thoroughly.

Now sprinkle the roasted cumin powder and lime juice and toss the salad well.

Serve garnished with coriander leaves.

Banana Cucumber Salad

Serves 2-3 Persons

Ingredients
2 bananas (*kela*), peeled, sliced
1 tbsp / 15 ml lime (*nimbu*) juice
2 cucumber (*khira*), small, peeled, sliced
2 green chillies, finely chopped
Salt to taste
2 tsp / 15 gm peanuts (*moongphalli*), roasted
and crushed
1 tbsp / 15 gm coconut (*nariyal*), fresh, grated
a few mint (*pudina*) leaves

Method
Put the sliced bananas into a bowl. Add the lime juice
to keep the bananas looking fresh or else they start
changing colour.
Mix the cucumber with the bananas. Then add the
green chillies, salt and crushed peanuts; mix well.
Serve on a platter sprinkled with grated coconut and
mint leaves.

White Radish Salad

Serves 2-3 Persons

Ingredients

1 radish (*mooli*), grated
1" piece ginger (*adrak*), thinly sliced
1 tomato, finely chopped
1 green chilli, finely shredded
1 tbsp / 15 gm coriander (*dhaniya*) leaves, finely chopped
Salt to taste
2 tsp / 10 ml lime (*nimbu*) juice
a few mint (*pudina*) leaves

Method

Squeeze the excess water out from the grated radish and put into a bowl.
Add the ginger, tomato, green chilli, coriander leaves and salt; mix well.
Add the lime juice and toss.
Serve the salad on a plate with ½ a sliced tomato and a few mint leaves.

Chickpea Salad

Serves 3-4 Persons

Ingredients
1 cup / 200 gm chickpeas (*kabuli chana*), boiled
1 potato, boiled, peeled, cut into cubes
1 tomato, cut into small cubes
1 green chilli, finely chopped
2 tsp / 10 ml lime (*nimbu*) juice
½ tsp / 2½ gm black salt (*kala namak*)
¼ tsp black pepper (*kali mirch*) powder
1½ tsp / 7½ gm roasted cumin (*jeera*) powder
Salt to taste
2 tbsp / 30 gm coriander (*dhaniya*) leaves,
finely chopped

Method
Mix the boiled chickpeas and potato together in
a bowl.
Add the tomato and green chilli. Mix the ingredients
well together.
Add the lime juice, black salt, black pepper, roasted
cumin powder, salt and coriander leaves; toss
thoroughly and serve.

Mixed Vegetable Salad

Serves 3-4 Persons

Ingredients

¼ cup / 50 gm French beans, washed, cut into small cubes
2 carrots (*gajar*), medium-sized, washed, cut into small cubes
1 capsicum (*Shimla mirch*), washed, cut into small cubes
1 broccoli, washed, cut into florets
1 cucumber (*khira*), washed, cut into small cubes
1 tomato, washed, cut into small cubes
2 onions, washed, cut into small cubes
½ tsp / 2½ gm black pepper (*kali mirch*) powder
2 tbsp / 30 gm coriander (*dhaniya*) leaves, finely chopped
Salt to taste
5 violet cabbage (*bandh gobhi*) leaves, washed
2 tsp / 10 ml lime (*nimbu*) juice

Method

Steam the French beans, carrots, capsicum and broccoli for 10 minutes.
Mix the cucumber, tomato and onions with the steamed vegetables.
Add the black pepper powder, coriander leaves and salt; mix thoroughly.
Lay the violet cabbage leaves separately on a plate and put the mixed vegetables equally on the leaves. Add the lime juice and serve.

Papaya Salad
Serves 2-3 Persons

Ingredients
1 papaya (*papita*), small, raw, peeled, grated
2 tomatoes, cut into small cubes
1 green chilli, finely chopped
1½ cubes jaggery (*gur*)
a pinch red chilli powder
a pinch salt
2 tbsp / 30 ml tamarind (*imli*) juice
½ cup / 100 gm peanuts (*moongphalli*),
roasted, crushed
a few basil (*tulsi*) leaves

Method
Mix the raw papaya, tomatoes and green chilli in
a bowl.
Now prepare the sweet syrup to be added to the
papaya. Heat the jaggery cubes in a pan till it liquifies.
Add the red chili powder, salt and tamarind juice; mix
well. Remove and allow it to cool and then add it to
the papaya mixture.
Add the roasted peanuts and toss the salad till
evenly coated.
Serve garnished with basil leaves.

Mixed Vegetables and Fruit Salad

Serves 4-5 Persons

Ingredients
1 bunch lettuce, washed thoroughly
1 watermelon (*tarbuj*), small, cut into small cubes
1 bunch green grapes (angoor), deseeded, halved
1 cup pomegranate (*anar*)
1 guava (*amrud*), halved, sliced
1 star fruit (*karmal*), sliced
4 baby corns, steamed, cut into small cubes
a few basil (*tulsi*) leaves
Salt to taste

Method
Keep the lettuce in cold water for about half and hour and strain. This helps the leaves to remain steady and crisp.
Combine the watermelon, grapes and pomegranate in a large bowl.
Add the guava and star fruit along with the baby corns and lettuce. Toss all the ingredients well.
Serve garnished with basil leaves. Some salt can be added, if required.

Soups

The benefits of healthy soups are many. To begin with, soups make a great nutritious meal. They are proven to support the weight loss programs; particularly vegetable-based soups as they combine with lots of key nutrients including vitamins and minerals, and, of course, they are low in calories. A very good option for good health as soups make you feel lighter. They not only nourish your body, but mind and soul as well.

Kairali's Vegetables and Fruits – help the body to acclimatize according to the various seasons.

Mulligatawny Soup

Serves 2-3 Persons

Ingredients
1 tsp / 5 gm coriander (*dhaniya*) seeds
1 tsp / 5 gm cumin (*jeera*) seeds
½ tsp / 2½ gm black peppercorns (*sabut kali mirch*)
1 dry red chilli (*sookhi lal mirch*), small
3-4 garlic (*lasan*) cloves
1 tsp / 5 gm ginger (*adrak*)
1½ tsp / 7½ ml vegetable oil
½ tsp / 2½ gm fenugreek seeds (*methi dana*)
6-8 curry leaves (*kadhi patta*)
1 tomato, sliced
2 tsp / 10 ml lime (*nimbu*) juice
Salt to taste

Method
Grind the coriander seeds, cumin seeds, black peppercorns, dry red chilli, garlic and ginger into a paste. Keep aside.
Heat the oil in a pot; add the fenugreek seeds and sauté till brown. Add the curry leaves and then the ground paste; fry till slightly brown.
Add the tomato and about 4 cups water; cook till the mixture thickens
Add the lime juice, season to taste and serve hot.

Spinach Soup

Serves 2-3 Persons

Ingredients
7 bundles spinach (*palak*), fresh, roughly chopped
½ onion, chopped
2 garlic (*lasan*) cloves, crushed
3-4 black peppercorns (*sabut kali mirch*)
a pinch nutmeg (*jaiphal*), for seasoning
Salt to taste
1 tbsp / 15 gm onion, finely chopped

Method
Steam the fresh spinach with onion, garlic and black peppercorns.
When cool, put the spinach in the blender and make a smooth purée.
Pour the purée in a pot, add some water and simmer for about 5 minutes. Season with nutmeg, salt and some onion; serve hot.

Tomato Soup

Serves 2-3 Persons

Ingredients

6-8 tomatoes, ripe, cut
1 onion, ½ roughly chopped and ½ finely chopped
1 green chilli, small
2 garlic (*lasan*) cloves
1" stick cinnamon (*dalchini*)
1 tbsp / 15 ml oil
4-5 curry leaves (*kadhi patta*)
¼ tsp black peppercorns (*sabut kali mirch*), crushed
Salt to taste

Method

Pressure cook the tomatoes with the roughly chopped onion, green chilli, garlic, cinnamon stick and 2 cups water till 2 whistles. Remove and keep aside to cool.
When cool, blend the mixture in a blender. Remove and strain.
Heat the oil in a heavy-bottomed pan; add the finely chopped onion and fry till golden brown. Add the curry leaves and pour in the tomato soup.
Serve hot seasoned with crushed black pepper and salt.

Mixed Vegetable Soup

Serves 2-3 Persons

Ingredients
½ cup / 100 gm carrots (*gajar*), chopped
¼ cup / 50 gm French beans, chopped
½ cup / 100 gm green peas (*hara mattar*), shelled
1½ cups / 300 gm tomato, chopped
1 tsp / 5 gm garlic (*lasan*) paste
1 tsp / 5 gm ginger (*adrak*) paste
¼ tsp black peppercorns (*sabut kali mirch*), crushed
1 tbsp / 15 gm coriander (*dhaniya*) leaves, chopped
Salt to taste

Method
Pressure cook all the vegetables with garlic paste, ginger paste and sufficient water till just one whistle is released. Switch off the gas and allow the pressure to release on its own.
Serve hot sprinkled with crushed black pepper, coriander leaves and required quantity of salt.

Soups

Vegetable-Oats Soup

Serves 2-3 Persons

Ingredients

½ cup / 100 gm onions, washed, finely chopped
3 stalks of celery, washed, finely chopped
1 cup / 200 gm French beans, fresh, finely chopped
1 cup / 200 gm green peas (*hara mattar*), fresh, shelled
½ cup / 100 gm oats
Salt to taste
½ tsp / 2½ gm cumin (*jeera*) seeds, roasted, powdered

Method

Combine all the vegetables together in a bowl.
Transfer them into a very large, saucepan. Add
6-7 cups water. Cook for about 30 minutes.
Now add the oats and cook for about 10 minutes
more. Add salt and when serving dress it with freshly
roasted cumin powder.

Okra Soup

Serves 3-4 Persons

Ingredients
12 okra (*bhindi*), washed, pat-dried, chopped into small pieces
½ cup / 100 gm French beans, washed, chopped
1 cup / 200 gm bottle gourd (*lauki*), washed, chopped
1 cup / 200 gm carrot (*gajar*), washed, chopped
½ cup / 100 gm onions, washed, chopped
2" piece ginger (*adrak*), chopped
1 garlic (*lasan*) clove
Salt to taste
1 tbsp / 15 gm black peppercorns (*sabut kali mirch*), crushed

Method
Put all the vegetables (except okra) into a pressure cooker with about 3 cups water. Cook well till 2-3 whistles are released.
Strain all the vegetables in a strainer and keep the stock aside. You could add some more water to this stock and bring to the boil.
Now add the cut okra to the stock and simmer for 5 minutes. Add salt to taste. Sprinkle some freshly crushed black pepper while serving.

Celery Onion Soup

Serves 6-8 Persons

Ingredients

10 red onions, small, 9 peeled, washed and sliced
2 celery stalks, finely chopped
3 garlic (*lasan*) cloves, chopped
1 **small piece** ginger (*adrak*), chopped
6 black peppercorns (*sabut kali mirch*)
Salt to taste
2 **tsp** / **10 gm** clarified butter (*ghee*)
¼ **tsp** lime (*nimbu*) juice (optional)

Method

Put the sliced onions in a thick-bottomed pan with
4 cups water.
Add the garlic, ginger and black peppercorns; cook for
about 10 minutes.
Remove from heat and allow it to cool. Put into the
blender and strain.
Add the celery to the onion stock and allow it to
simmer for about 10-15 minutes. Add salt and remove
from heat.
Take the last one onion and dice it into fine pieces.
Heat the clarified butter in a pan; fry the onion till
golden brown. Remove.
Serve the soup hot garnished with fried onion and a
dash of lime juice, optional.

Green Gram Soup

Serves 3-4 Persons

Ingredients

1 cup / 100 gm green gram (*moong*) with skin,
washed thoroughly
1 onion, chopped
2" piece ginger (*adrak*), chopped
1 green chilli, chopped
1 tomato, finely chopped
½ tsp / 2½ gm cumin (*jeera*) seeds, crushed
Salt to taste
a few coriander (*dhaniya*) leaves, chopped
½ tbsp / 7½ gm black peppercorns (*sabut kali mirch*),
crushed (optional)

Method

Drain the green gram and put into a medium pan with
about 4 cups water.
Add the onion, ginger, green chilli, tomato and
crushed cumin seeds; cook for about 20 minutes or till
the green gram is well done.
Smash the green gram well with a ladle and add
some more water till it becomes soupy. Add salt
and mix well.
Serve hot garnished with coriander leaves and crushed
black pepper, optional.

Ridge Gourd Soup

Serves 3-4 Persons

Ingredients

2½ cups / 500 gm ridge gourd (*turai*), washed, cut into squares
2 onions, chopped
2 garlic (*lasan*) cloves, chopped
4 black peppercorns (*sabut kali mirch*)
Salt to taste
10 mint (*pudina*) leaves, finely chopped, for garnishing
1 onion, finely chopped

Method

Put the ridge gourd into a pressure cooker along with onions and garlic.
Add the black peppercorns and cook with 2 cups water, till one whistle is released. Lower the flame and cook for another 10-15 minutes. Remove from heat and allow it to cool.
Then put into the blender and strain. You could add more water to get the consistency desired.
Pour the stock into a pan, add salt and bring to the boil.
Serve hot garnished with mint and onion.

Yellow Pumpkin Soup

Serves 4-5 Persons

Ingredients

2½ cups / 500 gm yellow pumpkin (*kaddu*), washed, chopped with skin into discs
1 onion, large
2 green chillies
1" piece ginger (*adrak*)
2 garlic (*lasan*) cloves
¼ tsp roasted cumin (*jeera*) seeds
Salt to taste
10 curry leaves (*kadhi patta*), finely chopped

Method

Put the yellow pumpkin in a pressure cooker along with onion, green chillies, ginger, garlic, roasted cumin seeds and 2 cups water. Pressure cook for about 10 minutes.

Take off the pressure and cool. Put into a blender. After it is well blended put it back on heat and bring to the boil. Season to taste.

Serve hot garnished with curry leaves.

Mains

M ain course is the most substantial course of the meal, and usually the heaviest.

It is usually accompanied with rice or various breads. Red rice is normally recommended as it is healthy and contains a lot of vitamins.

Breads that go with this meal should be healthy and nutritious. It should be made of ragi, rice, wheat or various pulses.

Main course can be accompanied with chutneys such as Indian gooseberries (*amla*), raw mangoes, coconut, etc. The main concept of this meal is to have variety in taste. By using seasonal vegetables not only is ones' hunger satiated, but also the body is kept healthy and in balance.

The endless combination of colours and taste required for a balanced diet are in abundance at Kairali, provided by the fruits and vegetables grown here.

Spinach and Green Peas

Serves 2-3 Persons

Ingredients

1½ cups / 300 gm green peas (*hara mattar*)
1 bundle spinach (*palak*), washed thoroughly, chopped
2 tsp / 10 ml oil
1 tsp / 5 gm cumin (*jeera*) seeds
½" piece ginger (*adrak*), chopped
4-5 garlic (*lasan*) cloves, chopped
2 onions, chopped
1 green chilli, chopped
1 tsp / 5 gm coriander (*dhaniya*) powder
½ tsp / 2½ gm red chilli powder
1 thick cinnamon (*dalchini*) stick, powdered
1 clove (*laung*), powdered
2 tomatoes, chopped
½ tsp / 2½ gm salt

Method

Heat the oil in a thick-bottomed pan; add the cumin seeds and sauté. Add the ginger, garlic, onions, green chilli, coriander powder, red chilli powder and powdered cinnamon and clove; fry for a few minutes.
Add the tomatoes and spinach; cook for 5 minutes. Cool and put in the blender.
Transfer the mix back into the pan. Add the green peas and about 1 cup water; add salt and cook for 5 minutes.
Serve hot.

> **NOTE:** Spinach is very low in calories and very high in vitamins, minerals and other phyto-nutrients. It is an excellent source of vitamin K, vitamin A, magnesium, iron, calcium, vitamin C, vitamin B2, potassium and vitamin B6. It is also a good source of protein, phosphorus, vitamin E and zinc. It contains a lot of fibre and has omega3 fatty acids. The various nutrients help in protecting against diseases.

Bottle Gourd and Green Gram

Serves 2-3 Persons

Ingredients

¾ cup / 150 gm green gram (*moong*) spilt, washed, drained
1 bottle gourd (*ghiya*), small, peeled, chopped
½ tsp / 2½ gm turmeric (*haldi*) powder
½ tsp / 2½ gm red chilli powder
1 tsp / 5 gm cumin (*jeera*) seeds
1 tomato, finely chopped
1 onion, finely chopped
2 green chillies
Salt to taste
For the tempering:
1 tsp vegetable oil
½ tsp / 2½ gm mustard seeds (*rai*)
1 dry red chilli (*sookhi lal mirch*), halved
a few curry leaves (*kadhi patta*)
2 tbsp / 20 gm coriander (*dhaniya*) leaves, fresh, chopped

Method

Cook the split green gram with bottle gourd, turmeric powder, red chilli powder, cumin seeds, tomato, onion and green chillies in a pressure cooker until one whistle. Remove and allow to cool. Add salt and stir.
For the tempering, heat the oil in a pan; add the mustard seeds. When they start spluttering, add the dry red chilli and curry leaves. Sauté for just a minute or until the red chilli changes colour to dark red.
Add the cooked bottle gourd and green gram to this; mix well.
Serve hot garnished with fresh coriander leaves.

Mains

53

Sambhar

Serves 2-3 Persons

Ingredients

½ cup / 100 gm green gram (*moong*), washed thoroughly
2 aubergines (*baigan*), small, cut lengthwise into 1" pieces
1 carrot (*gajar*), cut lengthwise into 1" pieces
½ tsp / 2½ gm turmeric (*haldi*) powder
1 onion, sliced
2 green chillies, chopped
1 tbsp / 15 ml vegetable oil
1 cup / 200 gm okra (*bhindi*), cut lengthwise into 1" pieces
lemon-sized tamarind (*imli*), soaked in 1 cup warm water, juice squeezed out
Salt to taste
1 tbsp / 15 gm *sāmbhar powder*

For the tempering:
1 tsp / 5 ml vegetable oil
½ tbsp / 7½ gm mustard seeds (*rai*)

¼ tsp asafoetida (*hing*) powder
1 dry red chilli (*sookhi lal mirch*), broken
8-10 curry leaves (*kadhi patta*)

Method

Mix the aubergines and carrot with the green gram in a pressure cooker. Add the turmeric powder, onion and green chillies with 2 cups water and cook. Allow just one whistle and switch off the gas.

Heat the oil in a pan; fry the okra lightly. Remove and put this into the cooker with the rest of the ingredients.

Pour the tamarind juice and allow the mixture to simmer. Add salt to taste. Add the *sāmbhar powder* and continue to simmer for another 5 minutes.

For the tempering, heat the oil in a pan; add the mustard seeds, asafoetida, dry red chilli, and curry leaves. Pour this into the *sambhar* and stir well.

Serve hot.

Avial

Serves 2-3 Persons

Ingredients

10 French beans, cut lengthwise into 2" pieces
1 banana (*kela*), raw, cut lengthwise into 2" pieces
½ **cup / 100 gm** ash gourd (*petha*), cut lengthwise into 2" pieces
½ **cup / 100 gm** long beans (*sem*), cut lengthwise into 2" pieces
2 drumsticks (*saijan ki phalli*), cut lengthwise into 2" pieces
½ **tsp / 2½ gm** cumin (*jeera*) seeds
2" **piece** ginger (*adrak*)
1 **cup / 200 gm** coconut (*nariyal*), grated
2 green chillies
2 **tbsp / 30 gm** yoghurt (*dahi*)
Salt to taste
20 curry leaves (*kadhi patta*), fresh
1 **tsp / 10 ml** coconut oil

Method

Wash all the vegetables thoroughly and put them in a heavy-bottomed saucepan. Add some water and cook for about 10 minutes or till the vegetables are done.
In the blender, blend the cumin seeds, ginger, coconut, green chillies and yoghurt to a paste.
Mix this paste with the cooked vegetables, adding the required salt.
Add the curry leaves and coconut oil on top and serve.

Cauliflower and Peas

Serves 2-3 Persons

Ingredients
1 cauliflower (*phool gobhi*), large, thick, coarse stem discarded, leaves removed, stem sliced into thin long pieces with florets intact
1 cup / 200 gm green peas (*hara mattar*), fresh
1 onion, chopped
1 green chilli, fresh, chopped
¼ tsp turmeric (*haldi*) powder
Salt to taste
1 tbsp / 15 ml vegetable oil
½ tsp / 2½ gm mustard seeds (*rai*)
1 tsp / 5 gm cumin (*jeera*) seeds
1 dry red chilli (*sookhi lal mirch*), broken into 2, seeds removed
1 stalk curry leaves (*kadhi patta*), fresh
2 tbsp / 30 gm coriander (*dhaniya*) leaves, fresh

Method
Break the cauliflower into florets. Wash thoroughly in running water and drain.
Put the cauliflower in a saucepan. Add the green peas, onion, green chilli, turmeric powder, salt to taste and 1 cup water. Cook on high heat and bring to the boil. Lower the heat and cook till the cauliflower and peas are done and the water has completely evaporated.
Heat the oil in a saucepan; add the mustard seeds. When it pops, add the cumin seeds, dry red chilli and curry leaves. Put in the cooked cauliflower and peas and stir well.
Transfer into a serving dish and serve hot garnished with coriander leaves.

Cabbage Thoran

Serves 2-3 Persons

Ingredients

1 / 400 gm cabbage (*bandh gobhi*), halved, cut into long, fine ½"-wide shreds, washed, drained
1 onion, chopped lengthwise into fine shreds
1 green chilli, chopped
½ tsp / 2½ gm cumin (*jeera*) seeds
2 tbsp / 30 gm coconut (*nariyal*), grated
¼ tsp turmeric (*haldi*) powder
Salt to taste
1½ tsp / 7½ ml vegetable oil
1 tsp / 5 gm mustard seeds (*rai*)
1 dry red chilli (*sookhi lal mirch*), halved, seeds removed
10 curry leaves (*kadhi patta*), fresh

Method

Combine the cabbage with the onion, green chilli, cumin seeds, coconut, turmeric powder and salt. Mix all these thoroughly and leave for about 10-15 minutes.
Heat the oil in a saucepan; add the mustard seeds. When it splutters, add the dry red chilli and curry leaves; stir till the chilli turns into a darker shade. Add the cabbage mixture and stir well. Lower the heat and cook covered. Stir once in a while and cook until the cabbage is barely limp.
Transfer into a dish and serve hot.

Mixed Vegetable Curry

Serves 2-3 Persons

Ingredients

1 potato, washed, peeled, cut lengthwise into 4 pieces, then crosswise into small discs,
5 French beans, washed, trimmed, cut into ½" pieces
1 carrot (*gajar*), washed, cut into 2"-long piece, each piece is cut lengthwise into quarters, each quarter diced minutely
1 tomato, diced into small pieces
1" **piece** ginger (*adrak*), diced minutely
1 green chilli, diced minutely
2 garlic (*lasan*) cloves, diced minutely
¼ **tsp** turmeric (*haldi*) powder
1 tsp / 5 gm coriander (*dhaniya*) powder
1 clove (*laung*)
1 **small** cinnamon (*dalchini*) stick
Salt to taste
1 tbsp / 15 ml vegetable oil
1 onion, finely chopped
10 curry leaves (*kadhi patta*)

Method

Immerse the cut potato in some water or else it will turn black.
Take a saucepan and add all the cut vegetables. Pour about 2 cups water. Add the turmeric powder, coriander powder, clove and cinnamon with the required amount of salt. When it comes to a rolling boil, lower the heat and cook, covered, till the vegetables are well done.
Heat the oil in another saucepan; add the onion and fry till dark golden brown. Add the curry leaves and stir for about 2 minutes. Pour in the vegetable curry; mix well. Serve hot.

Ash Gourd Curry

Serves 2-3 Persons

Ingredients

1½ cups / 250 gm ash gourd (*petha*), peeled, cut
lengthwise into ½" pieces, washed
¼ tsp turmeric (*haldi*) powder
Salt to taste
3 tbsp / 45 gm yoghurt (*dahi*)
½ tsp / 2½ gm cumin (*jeera*) seeds
2 green chillies
2" piece ginger (*adrak*)
1 tbsp / 15 ml vegetable oil
1 tsp / 5 gm mustard seeds (*rai*)
½ tsp / 2½ gm black gram (*urad dal*)
½ tsp / 2½ gm fenugreek seeds (*methi dana*)
1 dry red chilli (*sookhi lal mirch*), halved
2 stalks curry leaves (*kadhi patta*)

Method

Cook the pumpkin in a saucepan with about 1 cup
water. Add the turmeric powder and cook covered.
After the pumpkin is cooked, add salt to taste.
In a blender, blend the yoghurt, cumin seeds, green
chillies and ginger with ¼ cup water. Add this paste to
the cooked pumpkin. Bring the mixture to the boil for
about 2 minutes.
Heat the oil in another saucepan; add the mustard
seeds. When it splutters, add black gram, fenugreek
seeds and dry red chilli. Add the curry leaves; stir well.
Pour the tempering into the curry and serve with rice.

> **NOTE:** Buttermilk is light, sweet and sour. Regular
> use of fresh buttermilk tones the intestine and is very
> calming. It can cure mild cases of diarrhea. Yoghurt
> when blended with water converts to buttermilk.

NOTE: Red amaranth is rich in vitamins and includes various minerals such as calcium, potassium, iron, copper, magnesium and phosphorus. It contains large amounts of protein. Regular consumption of amaranth can reduce cholesterol levels and lower blood pressure. It helps in boosting the immune system.

Red Amaranth in Green Gram Curry

Serves 2-3 Persons

Ingredients
½ cup / 100 gm green gram (*moong*), washed 3-4 times
1¼ cups / 250 gm red amaranth (*cholai*), chopped
¼ tsp turmeric (*haldi*) powder
2 green chillies, finely chopped
1 onion, small, chopped
2" piece ginger (*adrak*), cut into fine discs
1 tbsp / 15 ml vegetable oil
½ tsp / 1½ gm mustard seeds (*rai*)
1 tsp / 5 gm cumin (*jeera*) seeds
1 dry red chilli, halved
1 stalk curry leaves (*kadhi patta*), fresh
Salt to taste

Method
Cook the green gram in a saucepan. Pour about 3 cups of water. Add the turmeric powder, green chillies, onion and ginger; cook over high heat and bring to the boil. Lower the heat and cook covered for about 10 minutes or till the green gram is done.
Remove the lid and add the red amaranth and cook for about 5 minutes.
Heat the oil in another saucepan; add the mustard seeds. When it splutters add the cumin seeds and stir. Add the dry red chilli and curry leaves; stir and pour this to the cooked dish. Add the required quantity of salt and stir well.
Transfer to a serving bowl and serve hot with chapatti or steamed rice.

Raw Banana Stem Thoran

Serves 2-3 Persons

Ingredients

500 gm raw banana (*kela*) stems, halved, cut into strips, then chopped into minute discs
¼ tsp turmeric (*haldi*) powder
2" piece ginger (*adrak*), cut into fine discs
Salt to taste
1 onion, chopped
2 dry red chillies
½ tsp / 2½ gm cumin (*jeera*) seeds
1 tbsp / 15 ml vegetable oil
½ tsp / 1½ gm mustard seeds (*rai*)
10 curry leaves (*kadhi patta*)

Method

Put the banana discs into a large saucepan with plenty of water. Take a fork and rotate it as if stirring the banana discs till all the strings gets entangled on to this fork. Discard the strings.

Wash the banana discs thoroughly and put into a saucepan. Pour about 2 cups water, add the turmeric powder and ginger; cook, covered, till tender. Add salt and mix well.

In a dry coffee blender, put the onion, 1 dry red chilli and cumin seeds; run on speed one for two seconds.

Heat the oil in a saucepan; add the mustard seeds, when it pops add the remaining dry red chilli and stir. Add the onion paste and stir till the paste is slightly brown in colour.

Add the cooked banana discs and stir well. Evaporate the water if required and add the curry leaves. Transfer to a serving dish and serve hot.

Ayurvedic
Herbal Diet for
Healthy Living

D iet plays a very important role to remain healthy and fit. The right diet has a powerful effect on the progress of not only the physical aspect of health, but the mental aspect too. A proper diet compliments the medicine, Ayurveda.

Excess weight is a problem which leads to various health disorders. Prolonged eating of heavy foods not only increases ones' weight, but also results in building up of toxins in the intestine and stomach and thereby not being able to absorb the nutrients from the food. Even cold, heavy food increases the fat in the body and according to Ayurveda, the *Kapha Dosa* in the body gets aggravated. Hence, one has to have a proper diet daily.

According to Ayurveda, one has to eat what is in season and live a balanced life in harmony with the changing cycles of nature.

One has to eat three substantial meals a day without snacking in between as the body has to do the function of burning the fat. Eating at proper times and at regular intervals with proper diet and disciplined regime is a must. This way the body gets enough time to burn the fat. Sitting and eating ones' meals is very important and not when one is on the move or is reading. One has to be relaxed and aware of what is going into the body and when in a relaxed state the digestive process is very effective and at its best. The digestive process is the strongest in the morning till afternoon; hence breakfast should always be taken and not skipped.

Using fresh ginger and spices such as fennel, coriander and cumin in food usually results in better digestion. Fresh curry leaves improve functioning of the stomach and small intestine. Water taken during meals should be boiled with herbs and had warm as they help in the digestive process.

Some of the herbal waters which can be had are cumin seed water, prunus cerasoides commonly known as *patumukham* in malyalam or Himalayan wild cherries in English and tribulus terrestris known as *nerinjil* in malyalam and land-caltrops in English. They help in the reduction of cholesterol, blood pressure and water retention in the body.

The lush gardens of Kairali is a feast for the eyes.

To make the herbal diet easy to understand and follow, a two week chart is prepared as ready reckoner. I have added roti or rice for dinner, but this can also be substituted for lunch depending on convenience.

All the gourd variety of vegetables contain almost 90% water and is very good for weight reduction. It has many health benefits and can be used as an important part of the diet. It is also good for the skin.

Losing weight, the Ayurvedic way, is healthy and holistic since it treats weight reduction as a lifestyle and incorporates a balanced diet of fresh and warm food. Crash diets are not a solution for long-term weight loss. Alcohol is strictly to be avoided during the weight reduction course. To remove the toxins that are accumulated in the stomach, certain herbal laxatives like *avipathy choornam,* etc., can be taken on the fifth, seventh and nineth day after dinner.

This fourteen days Ayurvedic diet if followed will not only make one feel healthy, but will also help to reduce one's weight substantially.

Left to Right: Navara Rice (Oriza Sativa) and
Warm Healthy Water to help in the digestive process.

BREAKFAST

1. Ash Gourd Juice with Ginger
Ingredients: ¾ cup / 150 gm ash gourd (*petha*), deseeded, cut into pieces
¼" piece ginger (*adrak*), finely chopped
Method: Blend both the ash gourd and ginger together. Strain and serve.

2. A Small Bowl of Pomegranate

LUNCH

1. Drumstick Soup
Ingredients: 3 drumsticks (*saijan ki phalli*), washed, cut into 2" pieces
2 cloves garlic (*lasan*), finely chopped
¼ tsp cumin (*jeera*) seeds, roasted, powdered
6 black peppercorns (*sabut kali mirch*), crushed
Salt to taste
3-4 curry leaves (*kadhi patta*)
Method: **Pressure** cook the drumsticks with garlic and about 1 cup water till well done. Once cooked, remove the drumsticks and squeeze out the pulp. Run the pulp and the water content through a strainer.
Heat the soup, add the roasted cumin powder, crushed pepper and salt. Serve hot garnished with curry leaves.

2. Cabbage, Onion and Cucumber Salad
Ingredients: 6-7 cabbage (*bandh gobhi*) leaves, cut into thin, long strips
½ onion, cut into thin strips
1 cucumber (*khira*), small, peeled, cut into thin strips
Salt to taste
¼ tsp lime (*nimbu*) juice
Method: **Mix** the cabbage, onion and cucumber together. Add salt and lime juice; toss well and serve.

DINNER

1. Vegetable-Oats Soup
Follow the recipe on p. 42.

2. Sprouted Green Gram with Carrot
Ingredients: ½ cup / 100 gm sprouted green gram (*moong*)
1 carrot (*gajar*), washed, peeled, grated
2 cloves garlic (*lasan*), finely chopped
¼ tsp ginger (*adrak*), finely chopped
4 black peppercorns (*sabut kali mirch*), crushed
Salt to taste
Method: **Heat** 2 tbsp water in a saucepan; sauté the garlic and ginger. Then add the sprouted green gram and carrot; stir for about 5 minutes. Add the crushed black pepper and salt. The dish is ready to serve.

3. Ragi Dosa
Ingredients: ½ cup / 100 gm Millet (*ragi*), soaked overnight
Salt to taste
Method: **Mix** the drained millet with about ¼ cup water and some salt. Put into a blender and make a smooth batter. Heat a non-stick pan and spread 1 tbsp batter over it. Allow it to cook on one side then flip over and cook till done. Serve hot.

BREAKFAST

1. Ash Gourd Juice with Gooseberry

Follow the recipe of Day 1 by substituting ginger with ½ piece of gooseberry (*amla*).

2. Watermelon with Mint and Ginger

LUNCH

1. Celery Onion Soup

Follow the recipe on p. 44.

2. Mixed Vegetables and Fruit Salad

Follow the recipe on p. 33.

DINNER

1. Bean Soup

Ingredients: 10 French beans, washed, cut into 1" pieces
2 cloves garlic (*lasan*), finely chopped
½" piece ginger (*adrak*), finely chopped
¼ onion, finely chopped
6 black peppercorns (*sabut kali mirch*), crushed
Salt to taste

Method: Put the French beans, garlic, ginger and onion into a pressure cooker. Add about 1 cup water and cook till 2 whistles are released. Allow the pressure to release and then blend the contents well in a blender. Strain and heat the soup. Add pepper and salt and serve hot.

2. Ash Gourd with Yam

Ingredients: ½ cup / 100 gm ash gourd (*petha*), peeled, deseeded, cut into square chunks
½ cup / 100 gm yam (*jimikand*), peeled, cut into square chunks
1 tomato, chopped into cubes
1 onion, chopped into cubes
2 green chillies, small, chopped
¼ tsp turmeric (*haldi*) powder
¼ tsp cumin (*jeera*) seeds
Salt to taste

Method: Cook the yam in a pressure cooker with 1 cup water till 2 whistles are released. Let the pressure release on its own, then add the ash gourd, tomato, onion and green chilies along with turmeric powder and cumin seeds. Pressure cook till one whistle is released. After the pressure is released on its own, add salt and serve with rotis.

3. Ginger and Coriander Chutney

Ingredients: ½" piece ginger (*adrak*), finely chopped
1 bunch coriander (*dhaniya*) leaves, washed, finely chopped
1 green chilli, finely chopped
1 small piece tamarind (*imli*)
Salt to taste
Method: Blend all the ingredients well together in a small blender till smooth. Serve.

4. Roti

Ingredients: 1 cup / 200 gm whole wheat flour (*atta*)
Salt to taste
¼ cup / 50 ml water
Method: Put the flour and salt in a mixing bowl. Add the water gradually while mixing everything together. Knead into a soft dough. Cover the dough with moist towel and allow it to rest for about 30 minutes.

Divide the dough equally into lemon-sized balls. Dip each ball into dry flour and roll out using a rolling pin. Heat a thick bottomed-flat pan on the stove, when hot, lower the heat to medium hot and put the rolled roti on it.

When light spots appear on one side flip the roti. When spots start appearing on this side too, flip the roti again to the other side; gently press the roti with a spatula all around. This will help the roti to puff up. Remove from the pan and serve hot.

BREAKFAST

1. Bottle Gourd Juice with Mint
Follow the recipe of Day 1. Substitute ash gourd with bottle gourd and ginger with 6-8 mint leaves.

2. A Small Bowl of Papaya

LUNCH

1. Banana Stem Soup
Ingredients: 6"-long banana stem, chopped into small pieces, washed under running water
2 cloves garlic (*lasan*), finely chopped
½" piece ginger (*adrak*)
1 green chilli
4 onions, small
1 stalk curry leaves (*kadhi patta*)
6 black peppercorns (*sabut kali mirch*), crushed
Salt to taste
Method: **Cook** the banana stem in a pressure cooker with garlic, ginger, green chilli and onions. Add about 1 cup water and pressure cook till two whistles are released. After all the pressure is released, put into the blender and blend well. Strain, warm the soup again; add the crushed pepper, salt and curry leaves. The soup is ready to serve.

2. Red Radish Salad
Follow the recipe on page 29. Here red radish is used which is chopped into 1"-long fingers, instead of white radish being grated.

DINNER

1. Yellow Pumpkin Soup
Follow the recipe on p. 47

2. Vegetable Sautéed
Ingredients: 1 onion, small, chopped into strips
½ cup / 100 gm ash gourd (*petha*), washed, chopped lengthwise into 1" strips
1 drumstick (*saijan ki phalli*), washed, peeled, cut into 1" pieces
6 okra (*bhindi*), washed, pat-dried, chopped into 1" pieces
7 black peppercorns (*sabut kali mirch*), crushed
Salt to taste
Method: **In** a non-stick pan, cook the onion with about ½ cup water. Add the ash gourd and drumstick; sauté. Place the lid tightly and cook for about 5-7 minutes. Then add the okra and sauté till dry. Add the crushed pepper and salt. Serve hot.

3. Roti
Follow the recipe of Day 2 on p. 75.

BREAKFAST

1. Cucumber Juice with Ginger
Follow the recipe of Day 1. Substitute ash gourd with cucumber.

2. A Small Bowl of Sweet Lime

LUNCH

1. Leek Soup
Ingredients: 1¼ cups / 250 gm leeks, chopped
1 onion, small, chopped
2 cloves garlic (*lasan*), chopped
½" piece ginger (*adrak*), chopped
1 green chilli, chopped
¼ tsp cumin (*jeera*) seeds, roasted, powdered
Salt to taste
Method: **Cook** the leeks, onion, garlic, ginger and green chilli with about 2 cups water for about 10 minutes. Remove and allow it to cool. Then pass through a strainer. To this add the roasted and powdered cumin and salt. Serve hot.

2. Carrot Black Currant Salad
Follow the recipe on p. 24.

DINNER

1. Carrot Soup
Ingredients: 1 carrot (*gajar*), large, washed, cut into small chunks
4 onions, small, chopped
2 cloves garlic (*lasan*), chopped
1 green chilli, chopped
Salt to taste
3-4 black peppercorns (*sabut kali mirch*), crushed
1 tbsp / 15 gm coriander (*dhaniya*) leaves, chopped, for garnishing
Method: **Cook** the carrot, onions, garlic and green chilli in a thick-bottomed saucepan with 1 cup water till the carrot is just tender enough to blend. Blend all the cooked ingredients together and transfer it back to the saucepan and warm. Stir for a minute or so, add salt and crushed pepper. Serve warm garnished with coriander leaves.

2. Bitter Gourd with Onion
Ingredients: 2 bitter gourd (*karela*), large, washed, cut into rings, deseeded
1 onion, large, cut into rings
a pinch turmeric (*haldi*) powder
1 onion, small
1 dry red chilli (*sookhi lal mirch*)
½ tsp / 2½ gm cumin (*jeera*) seeds
4 curry leaves (*kadhi patta*)
1 tsp / 5 ml vegetable oil
½ tsp / 2½ gm mustard seeds (*rai*)
Salt to taste

Method: Cook the bitter gourd and onion rings in a saucepan with 2 tbsp water. Add the turmeric powder and cook, covered, for about 10 minutes. Remove from heat. Now grind the small onion, dry red chilli, cumin seeds and curry leaves in a dry blender for a minute.

In another saucepan, heat the vegetable oil. Add the mustard seeds, when it starts spluttering add the ground paste and roast it for 2 minutes. Add the cooked onion-bitter gourd and salt, stir. Serve hot with rice or roti.

3. Coconut Chutney

Ingredients: ½ cup / 100 gm coconut (*nariyal*), fresh, grated
¼" piece ginger (*adrak*)
2 onions, small
1 tsp / 5 gm raw mango (*kairi*)
1 green chilli
4 curry leaves (*kadhi patta*)
Salt to taste
Method: Just put all the ingredients into a dry blender and blend well. The chutney is ready to serve.

4. Roti

Follow the recipe of Day 2 on p. 75.

BREAKFAST

1. Ash Gourd Juice with Gooseberry
Follow the recipe of Day 2 on p. 74.

2. A Small Bowl of Pomegranate

LUNCH

1. Tomato Soup
Follow the recipe on p. 40.

2. Drumstick and Onion Salad
Ingredients: 6 drumsticks (*saijan ki phalli*), peeled, cut into 1" pieces
1 onion, small, chopped lengthwise
¼ tsp cumin (*jeera*) seeds, roasted, crushed
¼ tsp black peppercorns (*sabut kali mirch*), crushed
Salt to taste
Method: Cook the drumsticks, covered, in a pan with about 1 cup water for 20 minutes. Evaporate it dry if any water content is left. Add the onion and mix well. Now add the crushed cumin seeds, black pepper and salt; toss well. Serve.

DINNER

1. Horse Gram Soup
Ingredients: ½ cup / 100 gm horse gram, soaked overnight, washed
½" piece ginger (*adrak*), chopped
2-3 cloves garlic (*lasan*), chopped
1 green chilli, chopped
1 tomato, chopped
1 clove (*laung*)
Salt to taste
Method: Transfer the horse gram into a pressure cooker with 2 cups water. Add the ginger, garlic, green chilli, tomato and clove; pressure cook for about 15 minutes. Allow the pressure to release. Add salt to taste and mix well. Serve hot.

2. Red Amaranth in Green Gram Curry
Follow the recipe on p. 62.

3. Roti
Follow the recipe of Day 2 on p. 75.

BREAKFAST

1. Oat Porridge
Ingredients: ½ cup / 100 gm oats, soaked in ½ cup water for 5 minutes
¼ cup / 50 ml milk
2-3 cardamom (*elaichi*) seeds, powdered
Honey to taste
Method: Take a saucepan, pour about 1 cup water and stir in the soaked oats. Cook on low heat for 5-6 minutes. Add the milk and stir well for another 2 minutes. Remove from heat and add the powdered cardamom and honey. Serve hot.

LUNCH

1. Green Gram Soup
Follow the recipe on p. 45.

2. Papaya Salad
Follow the recipe on p. 32.

DINNER

1. Okra Soup
Follow the recipe on p. 43.

2. Sprouted Lentils, Cooked
Ingredients: 1 cup / 200 gm whole green gram (*moong*), sprouted
1 onion, chopped
1 tomato, chopped
¼ tsp turmeric (*haldi*) powder
2 green chillies, chopped
Salt to taste
Method: Pressure cook the sprouted green gram till one whistle with ½ cup water. Allow the pressure to release on its own. Take a saucepan, sauté the onion and tomato with ¼ tsp water. Add the turmeric powder, green chillies and the cooked sprouted green gram; mix well. Add salt to taste and serve.

3. Roti
Follow the recipe of Day 2 on p. 75.

BREAKFAST

1. Cucumber Juice with Ginger
Follow the recipe of Day 1 on p. 72.
Substitute ash gourd with cucumber.

2. A Small Bowl of Papaya

LUNCH

1. Mixed Pulse Soup
Ingredients: 25 gm green gram (*moong*),
soaked overnight, washed
25 gm cowpeas (*lobhia*), soaked overnight,
washed
25 gm peas, dry, soaked overnight, washed
½" piece ginger (*adrak*), finely chopped
3 cloves garlic (*lasan*), finely chopped
1 green chilli, finely chopped
¼ tsp cumin (*jeera*) seeds
¼ tsp turmeric (*haldi*) powder
Salt to taste
Method: Pressure cook the pulses with
ginger, garlic, green chilli, cumin seeds,
turmeric powder and about 2 cups water
for about 15-20 minutes. Turn off the heat
and allow the pressure to release on its own.
Put the pulse mix into a blender and blend.
Strain, add salt and serve.

2. Sautéed Capsicum and Onion
Ingredients: 2 capsicum (*Shimla mirch*),
chopped into small squares
1 onion, chopped into small squares
2 cloves garlic (*lasan*), finely chopped
2-3 black peppercorns (*sabut kali mirch*),
crushed
¼ tsp cumin (*jeera*) seeds, roasted
Salt to taste
Method: Sauté the capsicum and onion in
a pan with ½ cup water for about 5 minutes.
Add the garlic, crushed black pepper,
roasted cumin seeds and salt; sauté for
another 5 minutes. Remove and serve hot.

DINNER

1. Beetroot Soup
Ingredients: 1 beetroot (*chukandar*),
small, washed, cut into small cubes
½" piece ginger (*adrak*)
2 cloves garlic (*lasan*)
Salt to taste
Method: Put the beetroot into a pressure
cooker. Add the ginger and garlic. Pour
about 2 cups water and pressure cook till
2 whistles. Remove from heat and allow
the pressure to release on its own. Pour
the beetroot mix into a blender and blend
well. Strain and add salt. The soup is ready
to serve.

2. Cabbage Thoran
Follow the recipe on p. 58.

3. Roti
Follow the recipe of Day 2 on p. 75.

BREAKFAST

1. Broken Wheat with Sprouted Green Gram

Ingredients: ¼ cup / 50 gm broken wheat (*dalia*)
25 gm sprouted green gram (*moong*)
1 green chilli, chopped
Salt to taste
1 tsp / 5 gm coriander (*dhaniya*) leaves, fresh, chopped

Method: Place the broken wheat and sprouted green gram with green chilli in a pan. Pour about 2 glasses of water and cook for 30 minutes on low heat. When cooked add the required quantity of salt and stir well. Serve garnished with coriander leaves.

LUNCH

1. Barley Vegetable Soup

Ingredients: ¼ cup / 50 gm barley (*jau*), washed thoroughly, soaked overnight
5 French beans, cut into small pieces
½ carrot (*gajar*), diced
¼ onion, diced
6 black peppercorns (*sabut kali mirch*), crushed
Salt to taste

Method: Pressure cook the barley with 2 cups water until one whistle is released. Lower the heat and allow to cook for another 15-20 minutes as barley takes time to cook. Add the beans, carrot and onion to the cooked barley and cook for another 10 minutes. Add the crushed pepper and salt. Serve hot.

2. Mixed Vegetable Salad

Follow the recipe on p. 31.

DINNER

1. Ash Gourd Soup

Ingredients: ½ cup / 100 gm ash gourd (*petha*), chopped
1" piece ginger (*adrak*), chopped
2 cloves garlic (*lasan*), chopped
¼ tsp black peppercorns (*sabut kali mirch*), crushed
Salt to taste

Method: Cook the ash gourd, ginger and garlic in a heavy-bottomed pan with 2 cups water. Cook covered for about 20 minutes. Remove the lid and smash the ash gourd well with a ladle. Add the crushed black pepper and salt. The soup is ready to serve.

2. Snake Gourd with Lentils

Ingredients: ½ cup / 100 gm snake gourd, peeled, cut into small cubes, washed
1 cup / 200 gm green gram (*moong*), washed in running water
2 green chillies, chopped
½" piece ginger (*adrak*), chopped
2 cloves garlic (*lasan*), chopped
1 tomato, chopped
¼ turmeric (*haldi*) powder
Salt to taste

Method: Put the snake gourd and green gram into a pressure cooker. Add the green chillies, ginger, garlic and tomato with the turmeric powder. Pour about 3 cups water and pressure cook till

2 whistles are released. Switch off the heat and allow the pressure to release on its own. Serve hot with the required quantity of salt.

3. Roti / Rice
Follow the recipe of Day 2 on p. 75.

BREAKFAST

1. Ash Gourd Juice with Ginger
Follow the recipe of Day 1 on p. 72.

2. A Small Bowl of Watermelon

LUNCH

1. Vegetable-Oats Soup
Follow the recipe on p. 42.

2. Gherkins with Cowpeas
Ingredients: ½ cup / 100 gm gherkins, washed, cut into thin round slices
¼ cup / 50 gm cowpeas (*lobhia*), washed
2 green chillies, chopped
½" piece ginger (*adrak*), chopped
2 cloves garlic (*lasan*), chopped
Salt to taste
Method: Cook the cow peas in a saucepan with about 2 cups water for about 20 minutes. Add the gherkins, green chillies, ginger and garlic; cook for another 10 minutes and allow the water content too completely evaporate. Add the salt and mix well. Serve hot.

DINNER

1. Radish with Leaf Soup
Ingredients: 1 radish (*mooli*), washed, cut into small pieces
1 green chilli, chopped
½" piece ginger (*adrak*), chopped
2 cloves garlic (*lasan*), chopped
4 radish leaves (*mooli ka patta*), finely chopped
¼ tsp cumin (*jeera*) seeds
Salt to taste
Method: Put the radish, green chilli, ginger and garlic into a pressure cooker along with cumin seeds. Add about 1 cup water and pressure cook till one whistle. Allow the pressure to release on its own. Put all this into a blender and blend well. Strain and pour into a small pan. Cook the radish leaves in the saucepan for about 3-5 minutes. Add to the soup. Season to taste and serve hot.

2. Grated Beetroot with Horse Gram
Ingredients:
½ cup / 100 gm beetroot (*chukandar*), grated
¼ cup / 50 gm horse gram, soaked overnight
2 green chillies
¼ tsp garlic (*lasan*), chopped
¼ tsp ginger (*adrak*), chopped
¼ tsp turmeric (*haldi*) powder
2 tomatoes, chopped
Salt to taste

Method: Pressure cook the horse gram with 2 cups water till done. In a saucepan, add the green chillies, garlic and ginger; sauté for about 2-3 minutes. Add turmeric powder, tomatoes, beetroot and cooked horse gram; mix well and cook for about 5 minutes. Add salt and serve.

3. Roti
Follow the recipe of Day 2 on p. 75.

BREAKFAST

1. Red Rice with Green Gram Porridge

Ingredients: ½ cup / 100 gm red rice, washed thoroughly, soaked in warm water for 1 hour
¼ cup / 50 gm green gram (*moong*), washed
¼" piece ginger (*adrak*), chopped
Salt to taste

Method: Mix the rice and green gram together. Add the ginger and 2½ cups water and cook. As soon as the content starts boiling, lower the flame and cook for about 30 minutes till the rice and gram are well cooked, almost mashed. Add salt and serve with mint chutney.

2. Mint Chutney

Follow the recipe of Day 2 on p. 75. Substitute coriander with mint.

LUNCH

1. Celery Onion Soup.
Follow the recipe on p. 44.

2. White Radish Salad
Follow the recipe on p. 29.

DINNER

1. Sago with Vegetables
Follow the vegetable-oats recipe of Day 1. Substitute oats with sago.

2. Cooked Mixed Vegetables

Ingredients: ½ onion, cut lengthwise
½ carrot (*gajar*), washed, cut into 1"-thin strips
6 French beans, washed, cut into 1"-thin strips
4 okra (*bhindi*), washed, pat-dried, cut into 1" pieces
¼ tsp turmeric (*haldi*) powder
1 green chilli, shredded
Salt to taste
1 tbsp / 15 gm coriander (*dhaniya*) leaves, chopped

Method: Heat 2 tbsp water in a non-stick pan; add the onion and sauté for 2 minutes. Add the carrot and beans; sauté for another 5 minutes. Add the okra, turmeric powder, green chilli and salt; toss all the vegetables well for 3-5 minutes. Transfer to a serving dish and garnish with coriander leaves.

3. Coriander, Ginger, Garlic Chutney

Follow the recipe of Day 2 on p. 75 of ginger, coriander chutney. Along with this add 2 cloves of garlic.

4. Roti
Follow the recipe of Day 2 on p. 75.

BREAKFAST

1. Bottle Gourd / Ash Gourd Juice with Lemon

2. A Small Bowl of Papaya

LUNCH

1. Cucumber, Gooseberry, Ginger Soup

Ingredients: 1 cucumber (*khira*), chopped
1 Gooseberry (*amla*), small, deseeded
½" piece ginger (*adrak*), chopped
Salt to taste
Method: Blend the cucumber, gooseberry and ginger together with about 1 cup water. Take a saucepan and pour the blended content into it and heat for about 5 minutes. Season to taste and serve hot.

2. Steamed Apple

Ingredients: 1 apple, medium-sized, peeled, cored, sliced
2 tbsp / 30 gm honey
Cinnamon (*dalchini*) powder to taste
Method: Heat 2 tbsp water in a skillet; add the apple and sprinkle the cinnamon, cover and place on heat and steam for 5 minutes. Transfer to a serving dish, add honey and serve.

DINNER

1. Carrot Soup

Follow the recipe of Day 4 on p. 78.

2. Spinach Sautéed with Onion and Cumin

Ingredients: ¾ cup / 150 gm approx spinach (*palak*), washed, drained
1 onion, medium-sized, chopped lengthwise
1 green chilli, chopped
½ tsp / 2½ gm cumin (*jeera*) seeds
Salt to taste
Method: Cook the onion in a saucepan with 1 tbsp water. Add the spinach, green chilli and cumin seeds; mix well. Leave on low heat for about 5 minutes. Season to taste and serve.

3. Roti

Follow the recipe of Day 2 on p. 75.

Herbal Diet

BREAKFAST

1. Ash Gourd Juice with Gooseberry

Follow the recipe of Day 2 on p. 74.

2. Sweet Lime and Pomegranate

LUNCH

1. Papaya Soup

Ingredients: 1¼ cups / 250 gm papaya (*papita*), chopped
4 cloves garlic (*lasan*), chopped
1" **piece** ginger (*adrak*), chopped
1 greenat chilli, chopped
1 clove (*laung*)
Salt to taste
Method: Put the papaya, garlic, ginger and green chilli in a pressure cooker with the clove. Add about 2 cups water and pressure cook till one whistle. Allow the pressure to release. Blend the contents in a blender and strain. Season to taste and serve.

2. Sprouted Green Gram with Carrot

Follow the recipe of Day 1 on p. 72.

DINNER

1. Clear Vegetable Soup

Ingredients: 10 French beans, chopped into small pieces
½ cup / 100 gm bottle gourd (*lauki*), chopped into small pieces
¼ cup / 50 gm ash gourd (*petha*), chopped into small pieces
2 cloves garlic (*lasan*), finely chopped
½" piece ginger (*adrak*), finely chopped
¼ tsp black peppercorns (*sabut kali mirch*), crushed
Salt to taste
Method: Pressure cook the vegetables along with garlic and ginger with 1 cup water until 2 whistles are released. Remove from heat and allow the pressure to release on its own. Put all the contents into a blender and blend well. Strain and add the crushed pepper and salt. The soup is ready to serve.

2. Banana Stem with Green Gram

Ingredients: ½ cup / 100 gm banana stem, chopped into small cubes
¼ cup / 50 gm green gram (*moong*), washed
2 green chillies, chopped
1" **piece** ginger (*adrak*), chopped
2 cloves garlic (*lasan*), chopped
¼ **tsp** turmeric (*haldi*) powder
Salt to taste
Method: Cook the banana stem along with green gram, green chillies, ginger and garlic in a pan. Add the turmeric powder

and about 2 cups water; cook covered
for about 20-25 minutes till soft. Add salt
and serve.

3. Ragi Dosa
Follow the recipe of Day 1 on p. 72.

BREAKFAST

1. Ash Gourd Juice with Ginger
Follow the recipe of Day 1 on p. 72.

2. A Small Bowl of Watermelon

LUNCH

1. Celery Onion Soup
Follow the recipe on p. 44.

2. Cabbage, Onion and Cucumber Salad
Follow the recipe of Day 1 on p. 72.

DINNER

1. Horse Gram Soup
Follow the recipe of Day 5 on p. 80.

2. Papaya with Ash Gourd
Ingredients: ¾ cup / 150 gm papaya (*papita*), chopped lengthwise into 1" pieces
¾ cup / 150 gm ash gourd (*petha*), chopped lengthwise into 1" pieces
2 cloves garlic (*lasan*), chopped
¼ tsp ginger (*adrak*), finely chopped
2 green chillies, chopped
¼ tsp turmeric (*haldi*) powder
Salt to taste
Method: Heat a saucepan and pour about 2 tbsp water. Add the garlic, ginger and green chillies and heat through. Add the papaya and ash gourd with the turmeric powder and simmer for about 10 minutes. Add salt to taste and serve.

3. Roti
Follow the recipe of Day 2 on p. 75.

BREAKFAST

1. Ash Gourd Juice with Mint
Follow the recipe of Day 1 on p. 72. Substitute ginger with 6-8 mint leaves.

2. A Small Bowl of Papaya

LUNCH

1. Cabbage Soup
Ingredients: 1¼ cups / 250 gm cabbage (*bandh gobhi*), chopped
1 onion, small, chopped
¼ tsp black pepper (*kali mirch*) powder
Salt to taste

Method: Put the cabbage and onion in a pressure cooker. Add the pepper powder and 2 cups water; pressure cook till one whistle. Allow the pressure to release. Transfer the contents into a blender and blend well. Strain, add salt and serve.

2. Gherkins with Long Beans
Ingredients: ¼ cup / 50 gm gherkins, cut into 1" strips
¼ cup / 50 gm long beans (*sem*), chopped into 1" strips
1 green chilli, chopped
1 onion, small, sliced lengthwise
Salt to taste

Method: Heat about 2 tbsp water in a pan. Add all the chopped vegetables and cook, covered, on low heat for about 7-10 minutes. Add the salt and serve.

DINNER

1. Bean Soup
Follow the recipe of Day 2 on p. 74.

2. Cooked Vegetables
Ingredients: 10 okra (*bhindi*), washed, pat-dried, chopped, halved
1 onion, small, finely chopped
¼ tsp cumin (*jeera*) seeds, roasted and powdered
6 black peppercorns (*sabut kali mirch*), crushed
1 small stalk curry leaves (*kadhi patta*)
Salt to taste

Method: Heat ¼ tsp water in a pan; add the onion and sauté for 5 minutes. Add the cumin seeds, crushed pepper and okra; sauté for another 5 minutes. Add the curry leaves and salt; mix-well and serve hot.

3. Roti
Follow the recipe of Day 2 on p. 75.

Herbal Diet

Herbal Therapies

Beside the Ayurvedic diet, Ayurveda also recommends various therapies. These therapies in combination with the diet will not only clean you internally, but will tone and rejuvenate your externally too. The therapies mostly done are Elakizhi, Udwarthanam and Navarakizhi.

Elakizhi: Fresh herbs and other medicated ingredients are used to prepare poultices. These poultices are warmed in medicated oil and the whole body is massaged. This therapy helps to stimulate the lymphatic flow and circulation aiding in the removal of unwanted stored water and toxins. Elakizhi stimulates the immune system to promote better health.

Udwarthanam: In this therapy, fine powder of various herbal grains are prepared and the body is massaged, the massage flow should always be in one direction, that is the upward direction.

Navarakizhi: In this therapy, massage is given to the body with poultices filled with cooked navara rice (*oriza sativa*), see note.

This exfoliates dull dry skin to retain its youthful appearance. It also eliminates dead skin cells leaving the skin feeling soft, moisturized and looking radiant. It is one of the most excellent form of therapies to impart luster to the skin and nourish the body through the skin.

> **NOTE:** Navara rice has antioxidant properties and are rich in minerals, iron and zinc. It rectifies the basic ills effecting the circulatory, respiratory and digestive systems. Navarakizhi is a treatment procedure for strengthening muscles and curing neuromuscular disorders. This rice can be consumed internally too and has been identified as a rice protein that is reportedly an anti-cancer agent, particularly effective against breast cancer.

Left to Right: Udwarthanam—Horse gram grains, one of the ingredients present in the weight-reduction powder. Elakizhi—Fresh herbal poultices.

© **Roli Books 2013**

First published in India by
Roli Books
M-75, Greater Kailash II Market
New Delhi-110 048, India
Ph: ++91-11-40682000
Fax: ++91-11-29217185

E-mail: info@rolibooks.com
Website: www.rolibooks.com

ISBN: 978-81-7436-962-8

Editor: Neeta Datta
Design: Bonita Vaz-Shimray
Pre-press: Jyoti Dey
Production: Shaji Sahadevan

Printed and bound at
Nutech Photolithographers, New Delhi